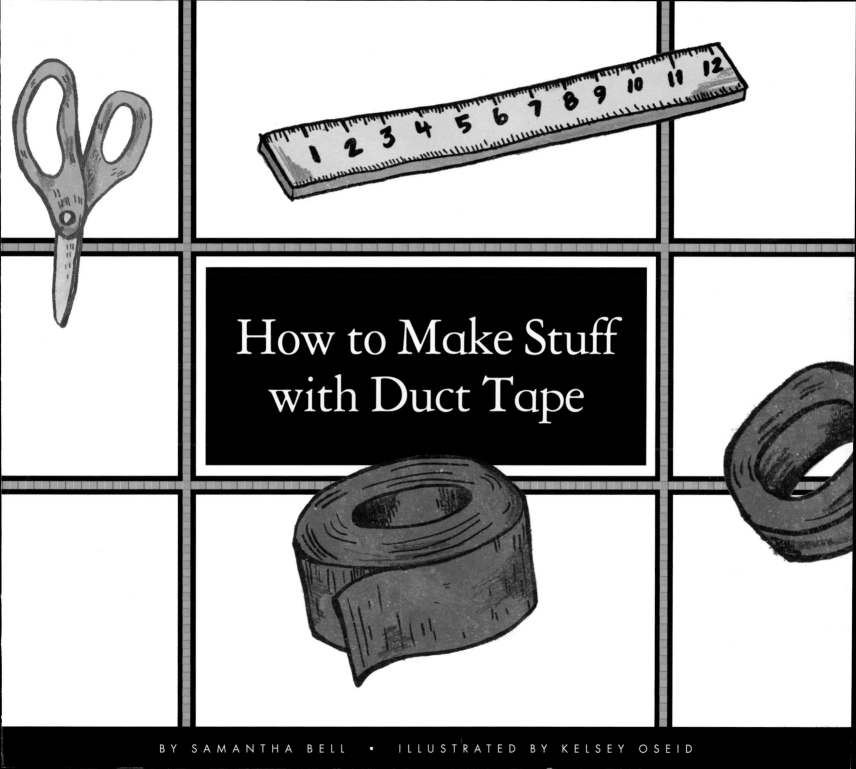

How to Make Stuff with Duct Tape

BY SAMANTHA BELL • ILLUSTRATED BY KELSEY OSEID

The Child's World

Published by The Child's World®
1980 Lookout Drive • Mankato, MN 56003-1705
800-599-READ • www.childsworld.com

Acknowledgments
The Child's World®: Mary Berendes, Publishing Director
Red Line Editorial: Editorial direction and production
The Design Lab: Design

Photographs ©: Feng Yu/Shutterstock Images, 4

ISBN: 978-1623235635
LCCN: 2013931352

Printed in the United States of America
Mankato, MN
January, 2014
PA02211

ABOUT THE AUTHOR

Samantha Bell is a children's writer, illustrator, teacher, and mom of four busy kids. Her articles, short stories, and poems have been published both online and in print, including magazines such as *Clubhouse Jr.*, *Learning through History*, *Boys' Quest*, and *Hopscotch for Girls*. She has also illustrated a number of picture books, including some of her own. For inspiration, she just has to turn to her family—there's always a story to tell!

ABOUT THE ILLUSTRATOR

Kelsey Oseid is an illustrator and graphic designer from Minneapolis, Minnesota. When she's not drawing, she likes to do craft projects, bake cookies, go on walks, and play with her two cats, Jamie and Fiona. You can find her work at www.kelseyoseid.com.

Table of Contents

Just Tape It!

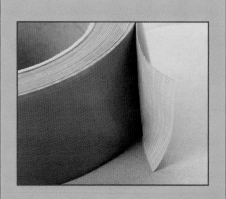

What is duct tape? Most duct tape is silver. But duct tape comes in many colors. Duct tape is super sticky. You can stick it to other objects. You can even stick it to itself. Most people use duct tape to fix things. But you can use it to make something new. This book will teach you how.

Talk to your parents before starting a duct-tape project. The projects in this book can be messy. But they are also fun!

Make sure you have all the right tools. Your parents can help you. For the projects in this book you will need:

- Duct tape
- Ruler
- Scissors
- Tin can
- Permanent marker
- Pen
- Jar lid
- Baseball cap
- Construction paper

Pencil Holder

WHAT YOU'LL NEED:
- Two colors of duct tape
- Ruler
- Scissors
- Tin can (peel off the label)

Follow these easy steps to make a case for your pencils and pens.

STEP
2

1 Start out with your first color of tape. Carefully cut a 10-inch (25 cm) piece of duct tape.

2 Repeat **step 1**. Now you have two pieces of duct tape. They should be the same size and color.

STEP 4

3   Wrap one piece of tape around the top part of the can.

4   Wrap the second piece of tape around the bottom part of the can. The two pieces of tape should be touching.

STEP 6

5   Next take your second color of duct tape. Repeat **step 1** with the second color.

6   Wrap the tape around the middle of the can.

Now you just need to fill your holder with pens and pencils!

- Duct tape (green duct tape looks great!)
- Jar lid
- Ruler
- Scissors
- Permanent marker

Duct-Tape Turtle

Turtles are **reptiles** that live in water. You can make your own duct-tape turtle!

STEP
1

1 Start by making your turtle's shell. Just cover the outside of the jar lid with duct tape.

2 Now cut two 10-inch (25 cm) pieces of duct tape. Stick the pieces together to make a duct-tape strip. The sticky sides should be touching.

STEP 4

3 Next you will make the turtle's head, feet, and tail. Draw five teardrop shapes on the strip. One shape should be bigger than the others. This is the turtle's head.

4 Next draw a triangle on your duct-tape strip. This is the turtle's tail.

5 Carefully cut out the shapes you drew.

6 Tape each shape to the bottom of your jar lid.

Now all you need to do is name your turtle!

STEP 6

Petal Pen

Do you have a **green thumb**? This project will show you how to make a green pen to go with it. Follow the steps below to write in style!

STEP
1

1 Let's start by making the **stem**. First cut a small square of white duct tape. Put it on the end of the pen. This is the flower's center.

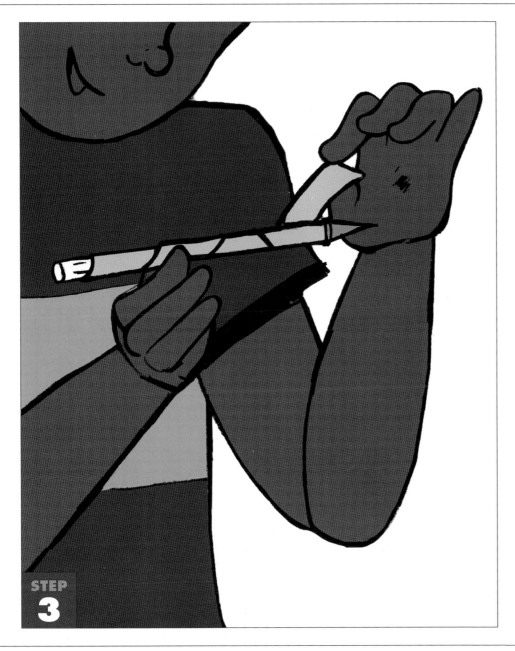

STEP
3

2 Now cut three pieces of green duct tape. Each piece should be about 1 inch (2.5 cm) wide.

3 Wrap the first green piece around the pen. It should touch the white tape. Now wrap the second piece around the pen. It should touch the first piece. Finally wrap the third piece around the pen. You are halfway to a flower!

4 Now it's time to make the **petals**. Start by cutting two pieces of red duct tape. Each piece should be 12 inches (30 cm) long.

5 Stick the two pieces together. The sticky sides should be facing one another. Cut five raindrop shapes from the strip you made. These are your flower's petals.

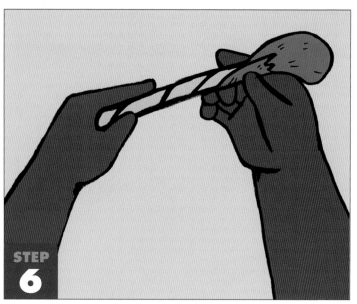

6 Cut a small piece of red tape. Use it to stick the bottom of one of the petals to the pen. Tape the petal where the white tape touches the green tape.

7 Repeat **step** 6 with each of the other petals. The edges of the petals should overlap a little bit.

8 Wrap one more piece of red tape around the pen. It should cover the bottom of all five petals.

9 Now gently bend the petals out to show the center.

Perfect! You made a pretty flower pen!

Duct-Tape Visor

WHAT YOU'LL NEED:
- Duct tape
- Permanent marker
- Scissors
- Construction paper
- Ruler
- A baseball cap

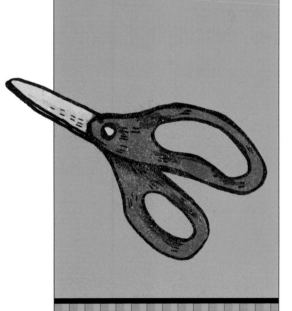

Stay in the shade with duct tape! Follow the steps below to make a hat to block the sun.

STEP 1

1 First you will make the visor's band. Start out by cutting two 12-inch (30-cm) pieces of duct tape. Fold each piece in half the long way. The sticky sides should be stuck together.

2 Now tape the two strips together end to end.

3 It's time to fit the band! Wrap the strip around your head. Ask a friend to tape the band together.

4 Next you need to make the bill. Carefully cut a piece of construction paper. The piece should be 6 inches (15 cm) wide and 8 inches (20 cm) long.

5 Now cover the paper with duct-tape pieces. This is a duct-tape sheet.

6 Next put the bill of the baseball cap on the duct-tape sheet. Line up the straight part of the bill with the edge of the duct-tape sheet. Trace the edge of the bill with your marker. Then cut along this line.

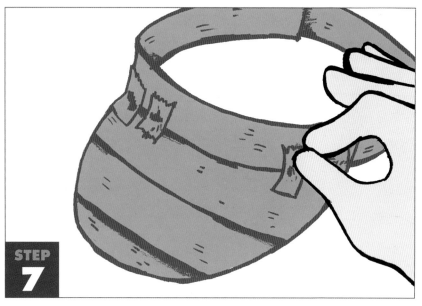

7 Now just tape the bill to the bottom of the band. Start at each outside corner. Work your way to the middle.

Now you can show off your new hat. Stay cool!

DRESSING UP WITH DUCT TAPE

Sometimes people use duct tape to make clothes. One brand of duct tape even has a contest. High school students can compete for a prize. Boys try to win by making duct-tape suits. Girls try to win by making duct-tape dresses.

Duct-Tape Wallet

WHAT YOU'LL NEED:

- Two colors of duct tape
- Construction paper
- Ruler
- Permanent marker
- Scissors

Learn how to make a duct-tape wallet. You can carry your money, library card, and more!

STEP 1

1 Begin by cutting a piece of construction paper. The paper should be 4 inches (10 cm) wide and 9 inches (23 cm) long. Cut another piece of construction paper. This piece should be 3 ½ inches (9 cm) wide and 9 inches (23 cm) long.

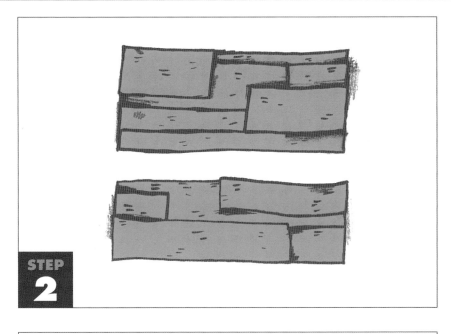

2 Next cover both pieces of construction paper with duct tape. Use the same color of duct tape for both. Now you have two duct-tape sheets.

3 Put the smaller duct-tape sheet on top of the bigger sheet. Line up the bottom edge and sides. Tape the bottoms together. Now tape one of the sides together. Tape only up to the top of the smaller sheet.

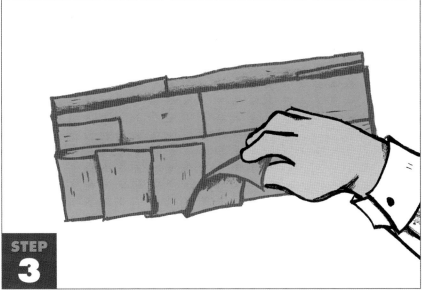

4 Repeat **step** 3 on the other side. You just made a pocket for dollar bills.

STEP
2

STEP
3

5 Now cut two pieces of duct tape. Each piece should be 4 inches (10 cm) long. Stick them together to make a duct-tape strip.

6 Repeat **step 5**. Now you have two duct-tape strips.

7 Put one strip on top of your wallet. Line it up with the bottom edge and the outside edge.

8 Tape the bottom and sides your strip.

9 Repeat **steps** 7 and **8** on the other side. Now you have two little pockets for cards.

10 Finally fold the wallet in half.

Make the wallet your own! You can use your marker to decorate the wallet.

NICE JOB!
The fun doesn't have to end! Read this book again. Try to think of ways you could change each project. You could give your visor duct-tape rabbit ears. Or make a duct-tape strap for your wallet. You could use markers to give your turtle a face. Be creative!

Glossary

ducts (DUHKTZ): Ducts are tubes used to move hot or cold air from one place to another. Duct tape was used to repair heating and air conditioning ducts.

green thumb (GREEN THUHM): A person with a talent for growing plants is said to have a green thumb. You can make a flower pen to go with your green thumb.

petals (PET-uhlz): Petals are the colored outer parts of a flower. You can make flower petals out of duct tape.

reptiles (REP-tilez): Reptiles are cold-blooded animals that crawl or slide on their bellies. Turtles are reptiles.

stem (STEM): A stem is the main, tall part of a plant that leaves and flowers grow from. A pen wrapped in green duct tape makes a perfect flower stem.

waterproof (WAW-tur-proof): Something that is waterproof does not let water enter it. Duct tape is waterproof.

Learn More

Books

Dobson, Jolie. *The Duct Tape Book: 25 Projects to Make With Duct Tape*. Richmond Hill, ON: Firefly Books, 2012.

Morgan, Richela Fabian. *Tape It & Make It: 101 Duct Tape Activities*. Hauppauge, NY: Barron's Educational Series, 2012.

Web Sites

Visit our Web site for links about duct tape projects: *childsworld.com/links*

Note to Parents, Teachers, and Librarians: We routinely verify our Web links to make sure they are safe and active sites. So encourage your readers to check them out!

Index